How to Simplify Your Life

Tips to Save Time, Money, and Stress

by
Kathy Peel

How to Simplify Your Life: Tips to Save Time, Money, and Stress
Copyright © 1994 by Kathy Peel

Unless otherwise indicated, all Scripture references are from the New International Version of the Bible, copyright © 1978 by the New York International Bible Society; used by permission.

Library of Congress Cataloging-in-Publication Data

Peel, Kathy, 1951–
    How to simplify your life : tips to save, money, and stress / Kathy Peel.
        p.   cm. — (Quick-me-ups)
    ISBN 0-8499-3573-3
    1. Conduct of life.   I. Title.   II. Series.
    BJ1581.2.P4277   1994
    170'.44—dc20   94-5468
                                                                                          CIP

Printed in the United States of America.

"There is a time for everything, and a season for every activity under heaven. . . ." —Ecclesiastes 3:1

Often when we read this verse we think about the seasons of the year, how they change, how we do summer things in summer and winter things in winter. Or maybe we think of seasons of death and life, a time to grieve and a time to dance, a time for war and a time for peace. But how often do we think of these words as daily words to live by? There is a time for every activity under heaven. All we need to do, with God's help, is figure out which activities we want to spend time on. We need to learn to live in God's time— to use the hours of the clock wisely to do what He created us to do. If God really wants us to do something, there will be time for it. On the other hand, if we think we want to do something, and we want to do it now, but we just can't get to it, maybe it isn't God's time to do it now.

I used to feel like a circus lady performing a plate-spinning act. One by one I spun my good china plates on the ends of broomsticks. Just when I got plate number ten spinning, I had to run across the room to rescue number one, which was about to fall. I could do it if I kept running really fast. But Ecclesiastes doesn't say anything about running really fast.

More than ten years ago, I decided I was running too fast and trying to spin too many plates. What this book is about is how—as a dual-career person, mom and professional—I began to figure out which plates I wanted to spin, what it was I wanted time for. Then I had to figure out how that affected my stress and cash level. Sure, I wanted to do more than any three human beings, and most of it might have been possible if I could afford to hire a full-time housekeeper, a nanny, a personal secretary, and three on-call general duty workers. But I couldn't. So back I went to the drawing board. Maybe I could have done most of what I wanted to do, even without a lot of extra cash, if only the kids never got sick, the roof never leaked, our cars never broke down, I didn't have to do things I don't like doing, and the world was a perfect place. So back to the drawing board again.

Once I figured out that what I needed in my life was to save time and money while reducing stress, so I could do the things that really counted, life got a little simpler. Not uninteresting, mind you, but manageable somehow. Maybe it was because I learned to ask God every day to help me find a way to conserve my resources so I could do what he created me to do.

Once I began to save time I found my life was less stressful. It can work that way with you too. If you do away with some stress-producing situations, you'll probably have more time. With less stress and more time, you'll probably make better decisions about spending money. When you have more money, you can spend it in ways to make more time, save your energy, and avoid more stress. It's like a three-ring circus that works to your advantage.

Sure, there are still plenty of days when I catch myself running ragged and have to stop, evaluate, and regroup. But I'm committed to discovering new ways to streamline my life, for my own sake and my family's sake.

Try these ideas and see if you don't begin to understand "there is a time for everything . . . ." Some ideas are for the bigger picture. Some address the small, simple details of daily life. I think you'll find, as I did, that honing, enhancing, and learning to make smart choices add up to significant savings of time, stress, and money.

TIME-SAVERS

⧗ Take a little extra time to do your work right. A sloppy or mediocre job may mean you'll have to do it over.

⧗ Ten minutes a day spent searching for misplaced items add up to over sixty hours a year. Don't put things down, put them away.

⌛ Listen to your biological clock and discover your prime time. What time of day are you at your best? When do you have the most energy? Do your most important work at that time.

⌛ Get out of bed thirty minutes earlier. If you get up thirty minutes earlier for a year, you add seven and one-half days of awake time to your schedule.

⌛ Edit your life. Drop nonproductive, time-eating activities.

⌛ Spend less unscheduled time at the grocery store. Shop for non-perishables every three months. Shop monthly for items that keep for a month in the freezer. Shop weekly for fruits, vegetables, and dairy products.

⌛ Take time to make time. Every minute spent planning saves three or four in execution.

⧗ Never dwell on failures. You can't do anything about them and they waste valuable time.

⧗ When a bill arrives, open it, put bill in mailing envelope, stamp it, and write the due date on the outside. Pay bills twice a month.

⧗ Keep presents for special occasions, wrapping paper and gift sacks, ribbon, and greeting cards on hand. You won't have to run to the store when you need to wrap a spur-of-the-moment gift.

⌛ Shop whenever possible by mail-order catalog instead of driving from store to store.

⌛ Write a travel checklist. List items to pack and things to do before you leave. Make photocopies and use one copy for each trip to save planning and execution time.

⌛ Always carry an extra key to your car and house. Calling a locksmith is time consuming and costly.

⏳ Consider writing a "not-to-do" list. Spend a day not doing these things that normally might rob you of time.

⏳ Keep a money bag of change and small bills for kids' lunch money and unexpected activities. Keep coins in your car for toll roads and parking meters.

⌛ To many people, minutes are like pennies—not worth picking up. But add them together and they become valuable. Instead of managing the day, try managing the minutes and see if you have more time to do the things you really want to do.

⌛ Buy clothing staples such as hosiery and underwear in bulk twice a year.

⧖ Keep your medicine cabinet well stocked. Middle-of-the-night drugstore runs are no fun.

⧖ Avoid wasting time sorting through junk mail. Write and ask the Direct Mail Association to take your name off the address lists they sell. DMA Mail Preference Service, 11 West 42nd Street, P.O. Box 3861, New York, NY 10163.

⧗ Save time making trips to the post office by purchasing a postal scale and keeping various types of stamps on hand.

⧗ Group knives, forks, and spoons together in the silverware container when loading your dishwasher. You'll save sorting time when they're clean.

⏳ Get to know a salesperson at your favorite gift shop that delivers. Have him or her keep your personalized gift enclosure cards on file, so you can simply call and have them wrap and send a gift.

⏳ Schedule family members' appointments back to back at the dentist or eye doctor. Have each person take something to accomplish while waiting.

⧗ Have a central location for extra keys. Use a key hanger or put tiny nails into the back of a cupboard door.

⧗ Write a family SOP (Standard Operating Procedure) manual. Create a logical system, schedule, or process for chores that recur on a regular basis. You'll save time and energy by figuring out how to do a job the best and most efficient way—then doing it that way every time, and family members will know whose turn it is to do what.

⏳ If you have to do a dirty job, dig your fingernails into soap beforehand so they'll be quicker and easier to clean.

⏳ When you store holiday decorations or out-of-season clothes in boxes, be sure to label each box and store it so that you can easily read the label.

⏳ Line the bottom of casserole pans with foil to save time scrubbing.

⌛ Keep your wristwatch and the clocks in your house five minutes ahead.

⌛ Double up on time. Exercise while watching TV, write letters while waiting for kids, or throw a load of laundry in while paying the bills.

⧗ Remember lost hours and minutes add up. Time management experts tell us that 20 percent of our time brings 80 percent of the results. Conversely, 80 percent of our time is virtually wasted on just 20 percent of our results.

⧗ Make a list of the things you want to accomplish every day and leave blanks to write in items that vary. Make photocopies of your list and fill one out each morning. Having a list will help you stay focused on priorities.

⧗ "Well begun is half done."   —Aristotle
Begin a new time-saving habit today.

⧗ Trade out chores with a friend with different abilities
and gifts than yours. If you enjoy working in the yard,
you can do the gardening for both homes. If she enjoys
housecleaning, let her do the interior chores.

⧗ Be a self-starter. "Go to the ant, you sluggard; consider its ways and be wise! It has no commander, no overseer or ruler, yet it stores its provisions in summer and gathers its food at harvest."—Proverbs 6:8

⧗ When cleaning house, carry a basket to pick up clutter and redistribute things to their proper places as you travel between rooms.

⌛ De-cluttering your house can save you time in the long run. Start with one room and sort through each drawer, closet, and shelf. Ask these questions about each item: Have we used it in the past year? Does it have monetary or sentimental value? Will it come in handy someday? If your answer to either of the first two questions is no, throw it away or pass it on. Regardless of how you answer question three, be ruthless and get rid of it. When you don't have to spend time cleaning or maintaining it, you'll be glad you tossed it.

⌛ Designate a special place to put items that need mending or fixing. Work on one item at a time when you have a few spare minutes.

⌛ Make use of small bits of time. If you wait for a large block of time to tackle a project, you may wait indefinitely.

⌛ Always take something to do in your briefcase or purse—reading material, stationery and stamps, or a small needlepoint project.

⧗ Edit your possessions. Weed out the things that are cluttering your life and wasting your time.

⧗ "Dost thou love life? Then do not squander time, for that's the stuff life is made of."   —Benjamin Franklin
Ask yourself often, "Is this the best use of my time?"

⧗ Don't waste time searching for lost school papers and forms. Designate a file for each child. When they come home from school have them place important papers, forms, and other school information in their files.

⧗ Cut down on ironing time by using fabric softener and not overloading perma-press clothes in dryer. When ironing a variety of items, start with things that require lowest heat and work up to the ones that require a hot iron. It takes less time for an iron to heat up than it does for it to cool down.

⧗ Learn something while you drive by listening to cassette tapes on a particular subject. The average American spends twenty-seven hours a year at red lights. That's a lot of class time!

⧗ Write an emergency list for babysitters and make photocopies. Include phone numbers for fire, police, poison control, ambulance, pediatrician, pharmacy, a neighbor who would help, and an in-town relative. Also list each child's name, birthdate, and blood type. Leave a blank space to fill in the number where you'll be.

⧗ Keep yard equipment and household appliances well maintained and ready for use the next time.

⧗ Shop for groceries when no one else is there—like early in the morning or late at night.

⧗ Always call for flight arrival and departure status before leaving for the airport.

⌛ Delegate personal clothes care to individual family members. A family of four does an average of one ton of laundry each year!

⌛ Cook and freeze in bulk—pancakes, waffles, biscuits, cookies, casseroles, soups.

⌛ Write facts you want to remember or interesting quotes in a notebook or on index cards. That way you won't have to search through whole books or magazines to find the information. Be sure to record the source.

⏳ "Take care of the minutes, for the hours will take care of themselves."

—Lord Chesterfield, letter to his son, October 4, 1746

Put this good advice to work in your life today.

⏳ Can't find time to exercise at the gym? Exercise to a workout video at home; wear tennis shoes when doing chores—bend, stretch, and move briskly; buy ankle or wrist weights and wear them when you're puttering around the house; do isometric arm exercises in the car when you're stuck in traffic.

⏳ Don't let phone calls interrupt your daily plan. Use an answering machine and return calls when it's convenient for you.

⏳ Turn off the TV and gain hours of extra time each week.

⏳ "Never have we had so little time in which to do so much."   —President Franklin D. Roosevelt
Stop, catch your breath, and analyze your schedule.

⏳ Buy a hand-held cordless vacuum to clean stairs in half the time.

⏳ Make use of direct deposit and automatic teller machines.

⏳ Play peppy music while doing a task. You'll move faster.

⌛ Don't obligate yourself to requests that don't fit your priorities.

⌛ If you have a computer modem, look into paying your bills electronically.

⌛ Let the kids help with housework. For example, make a cobweb pole by putting one thick cotton sock inside another and slipping them over the end of a yardstick, securing with a rubber band. Kids love trying to reach for cobwebs and dust in high places.

⌛ When you spend time playing, laughing, being creative, or relaxing, you'll renew your momentum, increase your alertness, and be able to get more done.

⌛ Every time you begin a task, ask yourself, "How important is this, and does it need to be done right away?"

⌛ Identify the time bandits and energy leaks in your life—phone calls, unplanned errands, searching for misplaced items.

⌛ "Teach us to number our days and recognize how few they are; help us to spend them as we should."—Psalm 90:12 LB
Look at each day as a gift from God. Ask him how he would have you spend it.

⌛ Put your suitcase out several days before a trip. Pack items you want to take along as you come across them.

⌛ Avoid pessimistic, whining people. They can drain you of time as well as energy.

⧖ Train your family to use the washer as a hamper for white clothes. Run a load when full.

⧖ "Time is money."   —Benjamin Franklin
Remember this when you're wasting time.

⧖ Use comforters and dust ruffles instead of bed-spreads. You can make the bed faster.

⌛ Consolidate errands and do them only on certain days.

⌛ Buy socks all of one kind and color for each child. This saves sorting time and you don't end up with extra socks with no matches.

⌛ Wash and use fewer towels. Monogram each child's name on a set of towels. Teach them to be responsible for hanging towel up to dry after use.

⧗ Bag your own groceries so you can put things together the way they go in your kitchen.

⧗ Eat a light lunch so you won't get sleepy and nonproductive in the afternoon.

⧗ When phoning someone you know is long-winded, call just before lunch or at the end of the day.

⏳ When your house gets out of control, walk through each room and write down all tasks that need to be accomplished. Post a list of specific cleaning assignments for each family member. Mark finished chores off the list. Reward yourselves when you finish.

⏳ Pour salt on an oven spill while it's still hot. It will take less time to clean when cool.

⌛ "Make haste slowly."   —Caesar Augustus
Practice this advice next time you feel like you have too much to do and not enough time to do it.

⌛ Run a warm iron over old contact paper to remove it more quickly.

⌛ Never walk from one end of your house to the other empty-handed.

⌛ Avoid backtracking. Divide your grocery shopping list into sections according to how your store is arranged.

⌛ Move your bedroom dresser close to your closet to eliminate steps.

⌛ To speed-clean a room, move in a circle around the room. Don't crisscross.

⏳ Store things as close as possible to the place where they will be used.

⏳ Create work centers with all the supplies needed for the task—bill-paying center, baking center, and craft center.

⏳ When running an errand, think of future errands you can accomplish at the same time. For example, when mailing a package at the post office, stock up on stamps while you're there.

⌛ Use a dustpan as a scoop to quickly pick up multi-piece toys.

⌛ Avoid making spur-of-the-moment trips to the store because you're out of something. When you open the last bottle or package of any item, add it to your grocery list so you won't forget to replace it.

⌛ Let younger children put an old pair of socks on their hands. They can wipe window sills, wooden shutters, and baseboards.

⌛ Make a list of things you can do when you have an extra five minutes—water plants, sew on a button, or straighten a drawer.

⌛ Evaluate how much time you spend on the phone "just chatting." This can be a big time eater.

⧗ Break down an overwhelming job into ten-minute segments.

⧗ Always make sure you have necessary cleaning supplies on hand. It's frustrating to muster up the energy to tackle a big cleaning project only to find that you don't have the right supplies.

⧗ Get the family involved in spring cleaning. Play "Basketball Clean-up." Station laundry baskets, clothes hampers, boxes, and trash cans in strategic locations around the house. Label each one and let the kids gently toss in clothes they have outgrown, as well as unbreakable items and trash. Designate one person to be in charge of sorting and folding.

⧗ Play "Beat the Clock" while working on a particular job. Set the kitchen timer and see if you can finish a task before the buzzer rings.

⌛ Write a list of questions and concerns before an appointment at the doctor's office. This way you won't have to call back to get answers to questions you forgot to ask.

⌛ Set up a color-coded filing system to fit the needs of your family. You'll avoid wasting minutes shuffling through useless papers looking for an important document.

⧗ Keep five files easily accessible in a file folder stand to use daily when opening mail. Place each piece of mail into one of the following files: Bills, Bank Statements and Financial Papers, Things To Do, Invitations and Personal Correspondence, and Reference. Toss everything else in the wastebasket.

⧗ Set aside a special time each week to do home office work. Treat this time as you would any important appointment.

⧖ Consider buying a home budget software system for your computer to help you keep track of finances.

⧖ The one thing we all have in common is twenty-four hours a day. If you're having trouble making choices about how to spend your time, keep a time diary for a week. Record how you spend every waking fifteen minutes. Now, what do you want to change?

⏳ Don't eat sugary snacks for quick energy to get a job done. They will give you a quick rush, but you'll feel worse in the long run.

⏳ Tackle the most difficult task of the day when you feel the most refreshed. You'll work faster and more efficiently.

⏳ Delegate whenever possible. You can't do everything, and someone else might like the job you hate.

⧗ One day each month don't schedule anything.
Just catch up.

⧗ Don't go to the bank or post office from noon to two
or on Friday afternoon. If you can't avoid the trip, take
something to do or read while you're waiting.

⧗ Know what you're fixing for dinner by midmorning.
Cook everything you can early. Late afternoon can be
the most hectic time of the day.

⧗ If you work outside the home, maximize the potential of your Crockpot and microwave oven. Set aside one day a month to cook in quantity and freeze.

⧗ Make use of delivery and cleaning services. They cost a little extra, but can save you time and money in other areas by freeing up your time.

⧗ Watch TV on your own schedule with a VCR.

⌛ Keep a project by the phone so you can work while talking.

⌛ Set the table straight from the dishwasher.

⌛ Put a long cord on your kitchen telephone or buy a cordless phone. Cook or clean up while talking.

⌛ Save clean-up time by using non-stick spray on any pan you bake in whether the recipe calls for it or not.

⌛ Quit buying things you don't need. Let everything you buy either replace or displace something you already have. Clutter is a time robber.

⌛ If you travel often, keep a prepacked overnight bag and toiletries ready at all times.

⧖ Learn to skim rather than read. The first and last paragraph, and the first sentence of each paragraph can tell you quickly if the material is something you want to read.

⧖ Always keep your car keys in the same place. Searching at the last minute takes time and produces stress.

⧗ Remember, less is more; don't waste time cleaning and arranging clutter. Throw or give away anything that isn't necessary, productive, or enjoyable.

⧗ Begin the habit of doing little things ahead of time. Tidy the house before going to bed; get spots out of clothing and linens before they set.

⧗ "Time is the most valuable thing a man can spend."
—Theophrastus
Let this principle guide your decisions.

⌛ Don't get sidetracked. If while cleaning out a drawer you find a scarf you borrowed from a friend, don't stop to call and tell her you found it, setting yourself up for a phone conversation. Return it when you finish your task at hand.

⌛ Manage your home like a business. Work smart.

⌛ When you feel cold or flu symptoms coming on, begin fighting the illness immediately. Call your doctor for medication and make adjustments in your schedule so you can get more rest. You can reduce sick time in the long-run if you listen to your body and respond promptly.

⌛ Plan your weekly housekeeping routine around your personal schedule and your biological clock. Doing chores late at night might make sense to you if you get a second wind after the evening news.

⌛ Don't schedule energy-draining tasks on days when you're tight on time.

⌛ "Lost time is never found again."—Benjamin Franklin

Stress-savers

When problems seem insurmountable, follow the advice Admiral Byrd used when his ship was locked in the ice of the Antarctic: "Give wind and tide a chance to change."

🂡 Don't let people "guilt" you into saying yes to something you don't have time to do. If you have trouble with this, don't give a reply immediately. Call back after you've practiced saying "No, but thanks for asking," in the mirror.

🂡 Plan one thing to look forward to each evening—working on a hobby, taking a walk with someone you love, or curling up in a quilt and watching an old movie.

💈 Listen to an inspiring message or relaxing music on cassette tape during rush-hour traffic.

💈 One thing we can always count on is change. If you're in the middle of a difficult situation, see it as a temporary stage in your life. Remember now is not forever.

💈 Display things around your home or work environment that bring fond memories to mind. Keep your favorite toys out. It helps to smile in the midst of daily routines.

⚎ Whether at work or at home, focus on positive things at mealtime. The brain creates body chemicals that counteract effective digestion when we worry, fret, argue, or process negative thoughts.

⚎ No matter what your career, do it with a sense of high calling. You influence the atmosphere and character of everyone around you, whether at an office, a plant, or at home. You are a very valuable person.

:: Don't sweat the small stuff. Choose your battles carefully, and save your time and energy for the ones that really matter.

:: Make laughter a priority. "A cheerful heart is good medicine, but a crushed spirit dries up the bones."
—Proverbs 17:22

⚙ Don't wait for a hard situation to completely turn around to change your attitude. Celebrate the first sign of positive change.

⚙ Go to a quiet place by yourself and evaluate your life. List three things that seem to cause the most stress in your life. Write down what you would like to change about them. Ask God to give you wisdom about what to do. It's a good idea to do this at least once a month, even if you're working with the same three stressors. Be patient with yourself.

🔢 Cluttered and messy work areas can cause stress and irritability. Block off a few hours on your calendar and use the time to clean up. Your time will be well spent.

🔢 Ask yourself, "What makes me feel energetic?" Make a list of these things for future reference. Promise yourself to make time for at least one of these things every day.

🎲 Be five minutes early for appointments. You'll have time to relax and compose your thoughts.

🎲 Give yourself the freedom to daydream. Astronauts in training at NASA are required to learn to daydream— an important skill for anyone who might need to think creatively in a stressful situation. They start off by day-dreaming for twenty minutes and build up to two hours.

When your children come home from school or you come home from work, schedule five to ten minutes of "reentry" time. Everyone needs to relax and acclimate before beginning end-of-the-day activities.

"I have been driven many times to my knees by the overwhelming conviction that I had nowhere else to go."
—Abraham Lincoln

See stress as a reminder to pray.

:: Give yourself permission to play and have fun regularly. It's good for your health, your productivity, and your personality. Go see a funny movie with a friend.

:: Take a long, hot bath.

:: Allow yourself at least one hour of uninterrupted prime time each day—quiet, uninterrupted time when you are most effective—to do a top-priority task.

⚌ When you're tempted to eat something gooey because you're under stress, reach for a piece of fruit instead, so you won't add guilt to your stress.

⚌ Take time to live, not just make a living.

⚌ Work smarter. Make lists for each morning, afternoon, and evening, and be sure to schedule time for play. Take the satisfaction of crossing things off. Don't do anything that isn't a dire emergency that isn't on the list.

⚏ Learn to say "I forgive you," while looking in the mirror.

⚏ "Do not wear yourself out to get rich; have the wisdom to show restraint. Cast but a glance at riches, and they are gone, for they will surely sprout wings and fly off to the sky like an eagle."　　　　　—Proverbs 23:4-5
Think about how really living these words might make a difference.

⚏ You can't do everything by yourself. Ask someone for help today.

:: Get up early enough to begin your day on a positive note. Mornings are the launching pad for your day.

:: Keep encouraging books that you can pick up for some quick inspiration around the office or home.

:: Read at least one chapter of the Bible every day. Take its strength and wisdom to heart to meet the challenges of the day.

👥 Carpool to work with someone you enjoy. Make a pact to focus your conversation on positive topics rather than problems so you both will start the day off right.

👥 Avoid morning chaos. Do as much as possible the night before. Make tomorrow's lunches while you're fixing dinner and store them in the refrigerator. Thaw juice in the refrigerator, set the table, and get out necessary items for breakfast, like the waffle iron and dry ingredients.

:: "You will keep in perfect peace him whose mind is steadfast, because he trusts in you."   —Isaiah 26:3 Think of God during the day.

:: Exercise relieves stress. Schedule some extra walking in your day. Park far enough away to give yourself a brisk walk to and from your office, the mall, or the grocery store.

⚡ "Fatigue makes cowards of us all." —Vince Lombardi
Get plenty of rest.

⚡ Tasks you don't enjoy tend to drain your energy. To compensate, add something you enjoy to the unpleasant job. For example, if you hate to pay bills, but you love Mozart and cinnamon coffee, put on a favorite sonata and brew a pot of fresh coffee before you start writing checks.

⛊ Fight perfectionism. Don't let anxiety about not doing a perfect job immobilize you.

⛊ If you feel like you're living in the fast lane, use all your gears—neutral, reverse, and low gear—to pace yourself throughout the day.

⛊ Remember, the real challenge is not to manage your time, but to manage yourself.

⚇ "In order to seek one's own direction, one must simplify the mechanics of ordinary, everyday life."　　—Plato
Ask yourself, "What's one thing I can simplify today?" Then do it.

⚇ Look your best. Getting into the rut of being sloppy in your appearance can drag you down and make you more susceptible to stress.

⚡ Be optimistic. Choose to dwell on the positive rather than the negative. Practice makes better in this, as in all things. When you find yourself thinking negative thoughts, stop and try to turn them around. Saying them out loud can help.

⚡ Create a stress-reducing house rule for everyone—Mom and Dad included—to reserve yelling and screaming for emergencies only.

▟▙ Turn off the TV. Constant noise causes stress.

▟▙ "Always take an emergency leisurely."

— Chinese Proverb

Don't panic. Break a rush job into its component parts.

▟▙ Avoid pessimistic people.

:: "The future is purchased by the present."

—Samuel Johnson

Do something today, like talk with your spouse about an annoyance before it gets out of control, to avoid stress in the future.

:: Don't be afraid to make mistakes. Mistakes are helpful in teaching us what works and what doesn't.

🎉 "May He give you the desire of your heart and make all your plans succeed." —Psalm 20:4
Instead of worrying about your plans and your schedule, write out your plans in a prayer journal and pray about them regularly.

🎉 Be flexible. The only thing predictable about life is that it is unpredictable.

⚡ Ask yourself, "What drains my energy?" Make a list of these things. What can you add or avoid?

⚡ Articulate your purpose. Write it down or share it with a confidante. Remember, if you are not controlled by your purpose, you will be controlled by your problems.

Ask yourself, "If I could, what work would I delegate?" Do it. If you're having trouble, you might want to ask God to help you be clear about how to delegate and about giving up control.

Be realistic about the amount of time a project will take. You're not superhuman.

Pray with an attitude of thanksgiving while you're doing an unpleasant chore. You might thank God for the privilege of taking a shower daily with warm water while you're cleaning the shower stall. Or thank Him that your family has clothes to wear while you're folding that mountain of clean laundry.

Avoid overwork and burnout. Schedule regular times to play.

⚏ Imagination is a powerful God-given ability. Use your imagination to picture what you'd look like and what you'd be doing right now if you were less stressed out.

⚏ Even though there will always be tasks in our lives that are less than exciting, remember that God's will is for us to find the work that brings to us the pleasure of doing what he created us to do.

◆◆ "I come to the office each morning and stay for long hours doing what has to be done to the best of my ability. And when you've done the best you can, you can't do any better. So when I go to sleep I turn everything over to the Lord and forget it."　　　　—Harry S. Truman
Do your work by this philosophy.

◆◆ Make a rotating schedule for the bathroom. Assign each family member a certain time, and put a clock in the bathroom. A makeup mirror in a teenage girl's bedroom can spare bathroom bickering.

⁇ Read *You Don't Have to Go Home from Work Exhausted* by Dr. Ann McGee Cooper, Bowen & Rogers.

⁇ "What then is the chief end of man? Man's chief end is to glorify God and to enjoy him forever."
—The Westminster Larger Catechism, 1861
Enjoying God means here and now too—your child's smile, the sun on your face, a rainbow.

:: Identify consistent conflicts in your home—how many minutes someone gets to play a video game, how much time is spent in the bathroom or on the phone. Meet together as a family and map out simple guidelines of fairness.

:: Don't take yourself too seriously. Tell a friend a funny story about something you did.

When your life is particularly stressful, call on a good friend to be a "stress buddy." Ask if you can call her just to be reassured that you're doing okay when you need to.

Cut back on caffeine. A brisk five-minute walk will give you a greater energy boost than a cup of coffee.

Look at your adversities as adventures. They can take you to new levels of growth and understanding.

:: "Keep your face to the sunshine and you cannot see the shadow." —Helen Keller

On a cloudy day, remind yourself of who and what made you feel like you're sitting in the sun.

:: Set a specific time for younger children to bathe, brush their teeth, and go to bed, so they'll have a sense of daily rhythm. Although they may stay up later on the weekends, don't alter the schedule greatly if you want the school-day routine to be easy to maintain.

🎵 Anticipate bedtime distractions. Make sure kids go to the bathroom before going to bed. Put a glass of water by the bed of a child who frequently needs a drink. Provide a night-light or flashlight for children who tend to be frightened of the dark.

🎵 Stress is what happens when we take our eyes off of God.

:: "Whatever you do, whether in word or deed, do it all in the name of the Lord Jesus, giving thanks to God the Father through Him." —Colossians 3:17

Remember that all of life is sacred, whether you're washing dishes, changing a diaper, or writing a sales contract.

:: Reward yourself with a simple pleasure after you've completed a task. Relax for a few minutes with a cup of tea and a magazine, or take a bubble bath.

🎲 Be as dedicated to planning fun times as you are disciplined about getting your work done. You'll have a tremendous boost in both energy and productivity.

🎲 Do your best, then await the results in peace.

🎲 "The best thing about the future is that it comes only one day at a time."　　　　—Abraham Lincoln
Take this to heart.

■■ Schedule some part of every weekend as a mini-vacation—even if it's just spending a few hours at a park away from the telephone.

■■ You do not stop playing because you grow old, you grow old because you stop playing.

■■ Seek out things that you enjoy doing, and find a way to enjoy what you do.

Always write down ideas and important information. This way you won't be frustrated when you forget something. Keep notepads in handy locations.

Ask kids to decide what they'll wear and set clothes out the night before. (Pack away all clothing that doesn't fit and put away out-of-season items to simplify decisions.) Have them put school gear in a designated place so they won't have to play hide-and-seek for books or gym shorts in the morning.

When you feel overwhelmed with all you have to do, think about these words of A. W. Tozer: "Keep your heart with all diligence and God will look after the universe."

Clarify on paper what tasks you're behind on and feeling guilty about. Tackle them one at a time.

Read positive material before falling asleep at night.

:!: Check the lighting in your work environment. Too little light can cause strain. Some people think fluorescent lighting causes stress.

:!: "Unless each day can be looked back upon by an individual as one in which he has had some fun, some joy, some real satisfaction, that day is a loss."
—Dwight D. Eisenhower
Reflect on your successes before you go to bed at night.

Before your feet hit the floor in the morning, begin by thanking God for the gift of a new day.

Keep an emergency makeup kit in your car or briefcase to quickly freshen up.

"Don't fret or worry. Instead of worrying, pray. Let petitions and praises shape your worries into prayers, letting God know your concerns. Before you know it, a sense of God's wholeness, everything coming together for good, will come and settle you down. It's wonderful what happens when Christ displaces worry at the center of your life."

—Philippians 4:6-7
The Message

Don't waste time beating up on yourself if you make a bad decision. Spend the time instead learning from your mistake. No experience is wasted if you come out wiser.

"Every man's work, whether it be literature, or music, or pictures, or architecture, or anything else, is always a portrait of himself."　　　　　—Samuel Butler
Does your work tell people you're stressed out? Take time to do your work in a way you can be proud of.

⚏ Pray the Serenity Prayer: God grant me the serenity to accept the things I cannot change, the courage to change the things I can, and the wisdom to know the difference.

⚏ Play calm background music while you eat. Research shows that listening to fast music causes us to eat faster and feel less relaxed.

If you have a huge project looming on your horizon, balance it by giving yourself the freedom to do something you've always wanted to do—just for fun. Sign up for dancing lessons, train for a race, enroll in a course at a community college.

Make a pact among family members to not call names, make unkind or cutting remarks, or use the phrase "shut up." Treating each other with respect reduces the stress level in a home.

🙂🙂 "Probably the greatest malaise in our country today is our neurotic compulsion to work."—William McNamara
Slow down. Do this for just one day. At the end, tell yourself how it feels.

🙂🙂 Keep a box of stickers, activity books, and small toys near the phone to positively distract a child when you have to make an important call.

:: If you take time off from work, really take the time off. Don't work on something else unless it's an enjoyable hobby.

:: Don't contaminate leisure time by focusing on problems or energy-draining issues.

⁈ When you feel overwhelmed with responsibilities, stop and ask Christ to make real in your life His invitation in Matthew 11:28: "Come unto me, all ye that labor and are heavy laden, and I will give you rest."

⁈ If given the choice at work of whether to take more time off or a pay raise, talk as a family about how you can cut back expenses so you can take more time off.

Keep a good novel going. Take a break and read a chapter in the midst of a stressful day.

Ease your morning. Make a checklist for yourself, noting appointments for the next day and items to take (cleaning, library books, show-and-tell items). Lay out your clothes and accessories. Establish a specific place for keys, glasses, purse, child equipment, and briefcase.

Purchase each school-age child an alarm clock. This helps kids take responsibility for their own schedules.

"Choose your rut carefully. You'll be in it for the next two hundred miles." —sign on an Alaskan highway
Are you in a rut? Do one thing differently today. Drive to work by a different route. Try something new on the menu.

⚏ Eliminate morning distractions. Don't turn on the TV unless an older child needs to watch a news report for a class. Allow playtime only after a child is dressed and ready for the day.

⚏ Allow enough time for an unrushed breakfast. Communicate as a family about the upcoming events of the day. Make it a point to speak positive, encouraging words to each family member.

Write down something you're worried about. What's the worst thing that can happen? And then what might happen? How unrealistic is your worry? Tear the paper up into small pieces and throw it away.

🎎 Designate a communications center in your home. Hang a bulletin board and family calendar. Assign a colored pen to every family member, and instruct them to write down their activities—sports, job hours, social events, etc. Create an in-box for each family member where others can deposit papers, mail, messages, and personal belongings. Have children clean out their backpacks soon after school and put pertinent papers and items in Mom or Dad's in-box. Check your box as soon as possible. Write down important dates, information, and make a to-do or to-buy list for each child's needs.

:: Share dinner responsibilities. One parent can cook while the other spends time with the children. After dinner, reverse roles. Let older children help with food preparation. Younger children can set the table. Everyone can help clear the table and clean up.

:: Reduce evening havoc by screening telephone calls. Teach a child to be the family receptionist, answering "Not interested" to solicitors, or "She'll call you back" to friends and business associates. Or turn on your answering machine.

📖 "God cannot give us happiness and peace apart from himself, because it is not there."   —C. S. Lewis Don't waste time trying to relieve stress in ways that are not pleasing to God.

📖 Learn to "just say no." Someone's need does not necessarily mean you are called to do it.

:: Add fifteen minutes of unplanned time to your morning schedule to cope with the unexpected.

:: Trust God. Remember He sees the whole parade, while we only see one float at a time.

Cash-savers

$ Use cloth napkins instead of buying paper napkins. This helps save money as well as the environment.

$ Share magazine subscriptions with a friend. Order different magazines that you both enjoy, then swap.

$ "Beware of little expenses. A small leak will sink a great ship." —Benjamin Franklin
If you can't figure out where your cash goes, keep a record for a month. Then you'll be able to make choices.

$ When traveling, ask hotels to give you a corporate rate. This rate—about 10 to 15 percent below the rack rate—is usually available to individual travelers.

$ Start a babysitting co-op. Establish a fair exchange system with other mothers who are willing to trade out keeping each other's kids.

$ Buy bargain tires marked "blems" for your car. They usually only have minor cosmetic blemishes on the sidewalls.

$ Grow your own flowers in season. Learn to dry them and make arrangements for the off-season.

$ "Riches are chiefly good because they give us time."
—Charles Lamb

Realize that saving money not only helps us live within our means, it can give us time.

$ Ask your local electric and water company to send a customer representative to your home to give you energy- and water-saving suggestions. Most will do this free of charge.

$ Carry a list of family members' clothing sizes in your organizer notebook or purse. When you discover something on sale, you'll have the information you need.

$ When traveling, don't charge anything extra to your hotel room. Pay cash instead. Verifying a list of room charges when checking out can be very confusing, and it's easy for hotels to make mistakes.

$ Don't wait for credit-card companies to lower your rates. If you want lower rates now, call customer service at the bank that issues the card.

$ Add a few drops of distilled water to makeup foundation to stretch it.

$ Instead of buying bags of ice, use empty milk cartons to freeze ice for keeping canned drinks cold in a cooler.

$ If your kids want something badly, let them earn the money to pay for half of it, and you pay for the other half. They'll appreciate it more and take better care of it.

$ Buy gasoline at stations that give a discount for paying cash. When you pump gas, check the air pressure in your tires. Underinflated tires reduce the miles per gallon your car will get on the road.

$ Change the oil in your car every three thousand miles and keep records. When you sell the car you can get a better price if the buyer knows it has been well maintained.

$ Split the cost and double your fun by vacationing with a family you enjoy with children close to the same ages as yours. Rent one large condo instead of two smaller ones. Share food costs and preparation chores.

$ Trade cuttings from favorite plants with a neighbor instead of buying new ones.

$ "You never know what is enough unless you know what is more than enough." —William Blake
Determine how much is enough for your family.

$ Store candles in the refrigerator. They'll last longer.

$ Go to matinee movies rather than prime-time, full-price ones.

$ Fix sack lunches for you and your kids. You'll save hundreds of dollars a year.

$ Nurture low-cost hobbies and activities, such as gardening, card games, walking and hiking, creating inexpensive crafts, taking picnics and exploring parks.

$ Clean your carpet yourself. Use club soda on spots, wait a few minutes then blot. For overall cleaning, ask a neighbor or two to split the cost of renting a carpet-cleaning machine for a day.

$ When shopping for large appliances, you can sometimes buy floor models at a reduced price.

$ Start a toy-swapping club with other mothers. Trade toys your kids don't mind living without for a couple of weeks. The kids will love having different toys often, and you'll save money not buying new ones.

$ Don't call a repairman immediately when electronic equipment or an appliance breaks. Many companies have toll-free numbers and can answer repair questions by phone. Call the "800 directory" (1-800-555-1212) for numbers.

$ Instead of buying a new couch, consider having your old one reupholstered. Check to see if there is an upholstery school in your area. Students take a little longer, but charge a fraction of the cost.

$ Save money by having your hair cut or your nails manicured at a beauty school.

$ Buy in bulk and stockpile any advertised specials your storage areas and budget allow.

$ Rewind rented videotapes immediately after watching and place in an easy-to-see location near the door. Avoid late charges.

$ Before buying new books, check to see if they're available at the library.

$ Supermarkets usually place the most expensive items at eye level, where they're more likely to be selected on impulse. Look at the entire group of products before making your decision.

$ Buy a matting knife and learn to mat and frame your own pictures.

$ Bury a piece of rusty metal under a plant instead of buying plant food. This will feed the plant minerals it needs.

$ Plan an inexpensive party. Ask your friends to bring food to share and a book or books to exchange. Everybody goes home with a "new" book. (You might also do this with costume jewelry or clothes with close friends.)

$ Instead of purchasing a step machine, buy a small stepstool with rubber tipped legs so it won't slip. Set aside regular times to step up and down one hundred times.

$ Brush your teeth twice a week with baking soda. This helps clean away coffee and tea stains so you can go a little longer between visits to the dentist.

$ Shop wisely for clothes. Stay away from fads. Good clothes with classic lines last a long time. The same holds true for purses and shoes.

$ Invite eleven other families to join a product-buying co-op; items can be purchased cheaper in large quantities. Each family takes a specific month to take care of shopping, dividing, distributing items, and collecting money.

$ Save money by learning to do things yourself. Check out "how-to" videos from the library.

$ Don't dry clean dusty curtains. Just run them through the dryer on fluff cycle.

$ Fresh flowers will last longer if you drop two or three pennies in the vase.

$ Make your own low-cost liquid wall-cleaning solution: 1/2 cup ammonia, 1/2 cup white vinegar, and 1/2 gallon water.

$ Check out local consignment shops before buying furniture or seldom worn clothing such as ski clothes, formals, and boys' blazers.

$ Enjoy low-cost family fun. Get up early, watch the sun rise, and cook breakfast out at a park. Go on a bike hike as a family, ride to a favorite eating spot, then ride back. Call your local parks and recreation department and ask about inexpensive programs and activities your family might enjoy.

$ "Put in its proper place, money is not man's enemy, not his undoing, nor his master. It is his servant, and it must be made to serve him well."   —Henry C. Alexander
Plan your spending and then don't worry.

$ Instead of buying an expensive new toy, entertain bored kids with a large box from a furniture or appliance store. They're usually free for the asking.

$ Check to see if there's a place near your home where you can pick large quantities of berries or fruit to freeze.

$ "No man can tell whether he is rich or poor by turning to his ledger. It is the heart that makes a man rich. He is rich according to what he is, not according to what he has." —Henry Ward Beecher

Do something today from your heart that will make you rich.

$ Take your own rafts and life jackets to water parks or the beach. Renting these items can be expensive.

$ Don't get caught in the trap of spending money on your children to ease the guilt of not spending enough time with them. Adjust your schedule and give them more of your time.

$ Hang a bulletin board at work for employees to post services or skills that they are willing to barter or to list used items they'd like to sell.

$ Instead of paying to board pets while you're out of town, ask a friend to come to your home to feed, water, and exercise them. Return the favor, and you both save money.

$ Lengthen the life of windshield-wiper blades by rubbing the edges with a knife. This exposes the softer material underneath and improves the wiping ability of the blades.

$ When planning a vacation, write to the Chamber of Commerce of your destination and ask for a map, free information about lodging and area activities, and discount coupons for local restaurants and amusement parks.

$ "Adversity reveals genius, prosperity conceals it."
—Horace

Let a financial setback reveal your creative genius. Brainstorm as a family about ways to make and save money. Many new businesses are created as a result of financial adversity.

\$ Drink water when you eat out at restaurants. This can add up to big savings if you have a big family.

\$ Resist the temptation to reach into the hotel in-room refrigerator for soft drinks, peanuts, and candy which usually cost several times the supermarket price. Bring your own snacks instead.

$ To avoid paying top dollar for convenience-store treats during gas and rest-room stops, pack a small cooler with travel snacks and drinks.

$ Sign up for airlines' frequent-flyer programs. Most offer tangible benefits—even to occasional flyers.

$ When you take children out to dinner, make sure the restaurant has a children's menu. (Some even have a kids-eat-free program.) An adult-only menu can run up the bill fast.

$ Shop hotel/motel rates carefully before making reservations. Use 800 numbers to compare room prices and amenities.

$ "Money and time are the heaviest burdens of life, and the unhappiest of all mortals are those who have more of either than they know how to use."

—Samuel Johnson

Ask God how He would have you use your money and time.

$ Look into taking a shuttle or public transportation to your lodging destination, then rent a car the next day—saving one day's rental cost.

$ Always inspect a rental car before driving. Report anything missing or broken immediately. Make sure the damage is noted on your contract so you won't get charged.

$ Fill the gas tank yourself before you return the car. Some rental companies charge for gas not according to how much gas the car actually takes, but based on how many miles you've driven—using a miles-driven/gas-charge conversion chart that assumes poor gas mileage.

\$ Consider vacationing at a national park. For campground reservations, call 800-365-2267.

\$ Let your teenager help you pay your monthly bills. This is usually an eye-opening experience and encourages frugality.

$ "Those who never think of money need a great deal of it."
—Agatha Christie

Practice thinking about money and making choices before you spend it, and give up worrying about it after you do.

$ Beware of buying or receiving anything that requires you to call a 900 number.

$ Never give out your credit-card number over the phone unless you initiated the call.

$ Share a membership to a discount grocery and supply store with another family.

$ Never forget your posterity is more important than your prosperity.

$ If you're so inclined, learn to sew. You'll save a lot of money on clothes and have the reward of creating something yourself.

$ Buy drink mixes rather than soda for children. Or mix fruit juice with seltzer water. It's a bit cheaper and healthier.

$ Buy used books.

$ "Simplify, simplify."   —Henry David Thoreau
Do you have things that require more upkeep than they are worth? Get rid of them.

$ Make rather than buy, Christmas and birthday presents. Involve your children. Particularly grandparents, aunts, and uncles will love some homemade treat or handmade present.

$ Mix your own baby food in the blender. Freeze it in ice-cube trays. It's cheaper and generally more nutritious.

$ "Look at the birds of the air; they do not sow or reap or store away in barns, and yet your heavenly Father feeds them. Are you not much more valuable than they?"
—Matthew 6:26

Pray using this Scripture verse during times when it seems that you can't make enough money no matter what you do. Trust God.

$ Start a gourmet club with friends. Take turns preparing fancy dinners rather than eating out at restaurants.

$ Learn to make your own potpourri. It's cheaper and makes an excellent gift.

$ Use store coupons. They add up over time. But beware of buying things you don't need just because you have a coupon.

$ Trade books or CDs or music recordings with friends. You not only save the cost of buying, but you experience the joy of getting to share and discuss your mutual tastes.

$ Rather than spending money going away on a romantic retreat with your spouse, trade babysitting weekends with a friend and have your weekend at home.

$ Use recycled paper for note and list paper.

$ Take your family's used clothing, books, toys, etc., to a consignment shop. Some will give you more dollars worth in trade than in cash.

\$ If you live in an area with major tourism, or business or education travelers, consider joining a home exchange for vacations. You open your home and you get to stay in a home rather than a hotel at your destination.

\$ "You don't seem to understand that a poor person who is unhappy is in a better position than a rich person who is unhappy, because the poor person has hope. He thinks money will help." —Jean Kerr

Remind yourself that money doesn't buy happiness—or peace of mind, love, or faith and trust. And let yourself laugh at your preoccupation with money worries.

$ Plan a family budget, including your older children in the process. You'll not only figure out how to live within your means, but you'll learn a lot about all your values and priorities and give your children an invaluable gift.

$ Take your own family photographs and mount and frame them for presents for friends and family rather than buying presents.

$ Pay bills on time and as much of the balance on your charge accounts as you can afford each month to save late fees and interest charges.

$ Keep exact tax records of tax-deductible expenses, particularly if you are self-employed or make money from a hobby. Checking with an experienced tax person can increase your deductions.

$ "The use of money is all the advantage there is in having it." —Benjamin Franklin
Make a list of the ways you use your money. Is there any unbalanced area? Do something about it.

$ If you can't afford to buy tickets to a special concert or play, find out if you can attend a rehearsal.

$ Avoid paying fines for overdue library books by writing the due dates on your calendar.

$ "Never respect men merely for their riches, but rather for their philanthropy; we do not value the sun for its height, but for its use." —Philip James Bailey
Find a ministry or charity you can help by sharing whatever riches you have—a little or a lot.

$ Call your insurance agent and ask for ways to decrease your premiums. Some carriers will give discounts for things like installing smoke alarms and taking a defensive driving course.

$ Avoid extra phone charges to your hotel room by making local calls from pay phones in the lobby for a quarter. Calls made from your room can cost up to $1.50 per call.

$ For the least expensive airline fares, make reservations as far ahead as possible.

$ Remember that banks and credit-card companies make mistakes. Check your bills carefully.

$ "Make all you can, save all you can, give all you can."
—John Wesley

Try to live daily by this simple strategy.

About the Author

Kathy Peel has built a national reputation as a family management expert with a sense of humor. The author of six books, including the best-selling *Mother's Manual for Survival* trilogy, *Parenting: Questions Every Woman Asks*, *Do Plastic Surgeons Take Visa?*, and *The Stomach Virus and Other Forms of Family Bonding*, she also co-produced the five-part seasonal *Holiday Survival* video series and is a regular contributing editor to *Family Circle* magazine. Kathy lectures frequently to conferences and conventions, has appeared on more than 250 TV and radio programs, and is featured in numerous newspapers and magazines. She has been married for twenty-two years and is the mother of three boys.